Awesome Adventures

Roger Carr
Kath Knapsey

sundance
A Haights Cross Communications Company

✖️ a black dog book

Published by Sundance Publishing
P.O. Box 1326, 234 Taylor Street, Littleton, MA 01460
800-343-8204

Copyright © text Black Dog Productions

First published 1999 as Phenomena by
Horwitz Martin
A Division of Horwitz Publications Pty Ltd
55 Chandos St., St. Leonards NSW 2065 Australia

Exclusive United States Distribution: Sundance Publishing

ISBN 0-7608-8036-0

Contents

Acknowledgments

Thanks to Dr. Phillip Law, Jesse Martin, Earle Bloomfield, Alex Bannister, and Jon Muir, who made writing this book an adventure in itself.

Authors' Notes

When I set off to explore the world, I thought it would take about six months. After four years, I came home again, but I'd still only seen a small part of what there is to see. I've rock climbed and scuba dived in Australia, canoed in Canada, hiked in Siberia, and skied in Scandinavia. But the biggest part of the adventure has always been meeting new people.

Kath Knapsey

I hope some of you who read these adventures will be inspired to plan your own. Don't hurry. It's best to plan them years ahead. Plan something that really interests you, something worth doing.

Roger Carr

Kath Knapsey worked at a variety of jobs before she discovered her favorite job—writing.

Roger Carr enjoys writing because it lets him be all of the things he could possibly want to be.

Introduction

There will always be people who want more out of life—brave people who seek out new places to explore. They choose to make a new path rather than follow a well-worn one. What makes them take risks? Curiosity is a driving force for most adventurous spirits. What is out there? Is there a better way? Can I do it?

It's this sense of curiosity that has led people to explore beyond the horizon. They may want to see what's on the other side of a mountain, like Alex in the adventure fiction book, *Crossing the Divide*. They may want to travel to the next continent or attempt to fly.

When explorers set out, there is an element of risk. Will the journey be difficult? Will they make it? What will they find when they get there? Sometimes it must seem as if the sensible choice would be to stay at home. But for some people, the risk becomes part of the reason that the journey is made.

Men and women have gone on trips of discovery to the most remote corners of the world. When they've climbed to the top or have been the first or the fastest, how do they feel? Do they feel like the greatest in the world? Or does it make them realize that they are a small part of a magnificent universe?

For all of their searching, perhaps the most important thing explorers find is what is in their own hearts. They find out how far their strength and courage will stretch.

To be an adventurer, you don't have to be big or strong. You simply have to have the courage to follow your dream.

Chapter 1: Introduction

Imagine . . .

that you are delivering mail by horseback for the Pony Express. You are tired, hungry, and on the lookout for danger.

THE HORSE was sweating, but the boy in the saddle was almost asleep. He had been riding for 7 hours through the night, and he was only 15 years old.

The rising sun appeared above the distant mountain range in the east. The long, dark shadows it created made confusing shapes on the well-worn trail.

The horse stumbled, and Josh jerked awake a moment to steady his horse and urge it on. Speed was everything. The mail must go through. But seven hours in the saddle was almost more than the boy could manage. And he had another two hours before he could rest.

Josh mumbled something to the horse. It sounded encouraging, although it really made no sense. But the horse responded by increasing its speed.

The horse had only another half hour or so before it could rest. But Josh would have to go on with a fresh horse for another 12 miles before his ride was finally over.

A sharp cry of warning from a frightened bird sounded in the boy's sleepy mind. He shook his head to try to waken himself. He was riding out of the woods now onto an open plain, and he looked around urgently.

The bird's fright may have been due to some prowling animal, or it may have been . . .

Josh's body turned cold with fear. Quickly his sleepiness vanished. He lashed at the horse as Comanche Indians swept in from the cover of the woods to his right.

"Go! Go!" Josh shouted.

The five Comanches yelled out their war cries and fitted arrows to their bows. They rode their ponies using only their legs to guide them, leaving their hands free to draw their bows.

Josh's steed felt the urgency of its rider. The horse's long, loping stride changed to the power and speed of a hard gallop as it raced along the trail.

Josh pulled out the heavy revolver from his belt, but held his fire. He did not want to upset the balance of his horse until he had to.

There was thunder on the plains now. The Comanches' ponies were adding their pounding hooves to the sounds of Josh's horse's racing stride. They came in at an angle toward young Josh, the Pony Express rider.

Just then, an arrow pierced Josh's hat, and it flew off his head. He did not hesitate, but pulled his revolver and turned to fire at the Comanches.

He used all six rounds, hoping to frighten them back. But they came on after him. He lay along the neck of his sweaty horse and rode hard.

At the next staging post, they heard the shots. No one waited to saddle up, but all leaped onto the closest horses and spurred them into action.

They swept out of the staging post. With their guns blazing, four riders raced for the dust cloud coming toward them. They were too far away to hit anyone, but the sounds from the guns had their effect. The Comanches turned their ponies away and headed for the cover of the woods. Josh rode on to the staging post and swung down from the saddle.

"I need a hat!" he yelled as he dragged the mailbags from his horse. Then he quickly threw the bags onto the fresh horse that was waiting.

He reloaded his revolver, snapping the empty shells onto the ground. Then Josh gulped down the drink someone handed him.

Someone else slapped a hat onto his head before he mounted. Josh reached down for the hunk of bread and meat someone held out to him. Then he took off on the new horse.

Ten more miles and he could sleep for a few hours. Then he would again mount a horse and begin the journey back.

With luck, he might even find his hat. . . .

Chapter 1

The Land

Exploring land almost always means meeting the people who live there. Whenever two cultures meet, at least one is changed in some way. The Native Americans who chased Josh in the opening story weren't interested in reading the mail he carried. They wanted to stop more white people from coming into their territory. The newcomers saw themselves as adventurers and explorers. But the people who were already there saw the strangers as invaders.

Raging Rivers and Sore Feet

In 1804, President Thomas Jefferson sent U.S. Army officers Meriwether Lewis and William Clark on an expedition across America. President Jefferson wanted Lewis and Clark to explore and chart a route from St. Louis, Missouri, to the Pacific coast.

impassable: Impossible to travel over or through.

It was to be a tough trip. They traveled on the rivers in small canoes. When rapids made the rivers impassable for the canoes, the team had to carry the boats and all of the equipment. This was made more difficult by the sharp, needlelike cactus spines that pierced through their thin moccasins.

When they went ashore to hunt, they were often chased by the grizzly bears they were trying to shoot. A member of the hunting party mistook Lewis for an elk because of the color of his clothes. Lewis was shot, although he was not badly hurt.

The members of the expedition needed to trade with the Native Americans along the way. Lewis and Clark hired a French Canadian trader called Toussaint Charbonneau and his wife, Sacagawea, as interpreters. Sacagawea was from the Shoshone tribe, and the expedition would be traveling through Shoshone territory.

Although she hadn't lived in that territory for many years, Sacagawea remembered many of the trails in her homeland. The expedition met a group of Shoshone warriors. In an amazing coincidence, it turned out that their leader was Chief Cameahwait, Sacagawea's brother. It must have been a wonderful reunion. Sacagawea translated and helped to organize a trade so Lewis and Clark could get horses from the Shoshone people.

Peaceful Mother and Child

When Native Americans went to war, they never traveled with women, especially women carrying babies. Shortly after she joined the expedition, Sacagawea had a baby. Having Sacagawea and her baby on the trip showed the Native Americans that the explorers were peaceful. So, even when Sacagawea couldn't translate native languages, she made it easier for the explorers to travel. Many of the Native Americans whom the expedition met further west had never seen white men before.

Sacagawea was the only woman among 33 men on the team. She cooked, washed, and mended clothes for the men. With her knowledge of the land and plants she was able to help the men find food and medicine. On one occasion when the team was traveling down the river in canoes, a canoe tipped over. Sacagawea was able to right the canoe and retrieve the supplies and expedition journals.

A Whale of a Trip

The Lewis and Clark expedition finished at Fort Clatsop in what is now Oregon. There, the team heard that there was a whale stranded on the beach. The men then set off to try to get some of its meat and oil. Sacagawea insisted that she join them. She didn't think it was fair to come so far and not see "the great water . . . and monstrous fish." Eventually, Sacagawea saw the Pacific Ocean. She may have traveled a greater distance than any Native American before her.

At the end of the expedition, Charbonneau was paid with money and land. Sacagawea received nothing for her valuable contribution.

Marco Polo, World Explorer

Marco Polo lived in Italy in the 13th century. When he was 17, Marco went on a trading trip with his father and uncle. They didn't come home for 24 years.

The party set out for China in 1271. They wanted to travel from Persia to China by ship but found the available vessels unseaworthy. They complained that the ships looked as if they were put together with twine instead of iron nails. So they set out by land. Through salty deserts to the Pamir mountain range and then to the Gobi Desert, they traveled on. Eventually they arrived at the court of the Chinese emperor Kublai Khan.

twine: A string made of several strands.

The trip had taken three and a half years. The Polos spent the next 18 years working for the khan and traveling in the region. The Polo expedition didn't return to Italy until 1295. The jewels that Kublai Khan had given them made them rich men. Marco Polo was the first Western European to travel across Asia. He traveled through Siberia, Mongolia, India, and Indonesia.

Who Would Believe It?

When Marco Polo eventually wrote about his adventures, many people thought he was making things up. It was hard for them to imagine white bears, people who rode animals called reindeer, and dogs pulling sleds. His stories had people scoffing. How could paper money be used instead of the gold and jewels that were used in Europe? Marco had seen many amazing things, including a palace made of reeds and held together by silk cord. It belonged to Kublai Khan and could be taken apart and moved when the khan moved.

scoffing: Making fun in disbelief.

One of the last things Marco Polo said before he died was, "I didn't tell half of what I saw because no one would have believed me."

The Hunt for Riches

Many Europeans thought of travel as a way of finding new resources to bring back to Europe. There was little awareness that other people might not want to have their possessions taken or traded. Travel was also seen as a way of spreading Christianity. It didn't matter that other cultures had religions that were as important to them as Christianity was to Europeans.

In 1532, when the Spaniard Francisco Pizarro met Inca prince Atahulpa, a priest handed the prince a Bible. He demanded that the prince listen to the word of God. Atahulpa threw the Bible down, replying that God wasn't saying anything.

Throughout Central and South America, Spanish conquistadors attacked cities so they could take the people's gold, silver, and jewels.

A group of conquistadors traveling in the Amazon rain forest met some native people. The conquistadors asked what was on the other side of the huge river. The natives couldn't tell them— probably because the river was so big that they'd never been across it. So the conquistadors killed the native people.

conquistadors: Spanish conquerors of Mexico and Peru in the 16th century.

Taking More Than They Needed

The same conquistadors stumbled across a food supply of turtles belonging to native people in the Amazon. The conquistadors did not offer to trade or take only enough to feed themselves. Instead, the men took "enough to feed 1,000 men for a year." No wonder they were attacked by angry natives during the rest of their trip down the Amazon River.

Ida Pfeiffer, World Traveler

Many women became great explorers and travelers even though it wasn't considered a proper thing for a lady to do. Before 1900, most women weren't allowed to vote, enter politics, or study at a university. Upper- and middle-class women were expected to work in the house and garden and to look after the children.

In 1842, Ida Pfeiffer decided to travel. She was 45 years old, divorced, and her sons were grown up. Of course, her family didn't approve of her traveling alone, but she went anyway. Often she dressed as a man so she would attract less attention.

Over the next 15 years, she journeyed to Turkey, Egypt, Iceland, Brazil, China, India, Iraq, Russia,

Europe, Southeast Asia, and the region now known as Israel. Writing books and articles kept Pfeiffer's bank balance healthy. She traveled through Iceland, to the rain forests of Brazil, and to Russia. In Russia, Pfeiffer was arrested on suspicion of being a spy. But she was soon released.

In 1852, Pfeiffer visited Borneo. She found that the forests there were home to some very strange animals, such as the orangutan. Next, Pfeiffer visited the Batak people of Indonesia. There was always the danger that she would offend the native people and be killed, but eventually she left safely. Ida Pfeiffer was the first person to be allowed to record the Batak's way of life.

Annie Royle Taylor

Annie Royle Taylor was a sickly child with a weak heart. As an adult, Annie got tuberculosis. She doesn't sound like much of an adventurer, does she? Yet, she was the first European woman to see Tibet. Taylor desperately wanted to see the holy city of

tuberculosis:
A disease of
the lungs.

Lhasa, which foreigners were not allowed to visit.

Like Ida Pfeiffer, Annie Taylor usually dressed as a man to make it easier to get around. For one thing, it meant that she could ride a horse with a leg on each side of the animal. Back in England, women were still expected to ride sidesaddle. This meant that they wore skirts and rode with both of their legs on the same side of the horse. Even when Taylor dressed as a woman, there was some confusion. At the time, women in Tibet pierced their ears. Because Taylor didn't, many people assumed she was a man.

On her way across a mountain range between China and Tibet, Taylor's small team was attacked by robbers. They took most of the team's possessions. One of her guides ran away, and another froze to death. Most of her horses froze to death, too. It was so cold, she wrote, "If boiling tea is not drunk right away, it freezes over." Taylor was only three days away from Lhasa when soldiers came to keep her from entering the holy city. She had to return to China. In 7 months, Annie Taylor had traveled 1,300 miles (2,100 km) on foot and horseback.

Margaret Mead, Anthropologist

Margaret Mead was a world-famous American anthropologist. She had an open, curious mind and a spirit of adventure. Throughout her career, she traveled extensively. She wanted to study how different cultures influence the behavior and personality of the people living in them.

In 1925, after graduating from Barnard College, Mead traveled to Samoa. There she studied the lives of adolescent girls. She wrote a book called *Coming of Age in Samoa*. It compared growing up as an adolescent in a Samoan village to growing up in Western societies. She observed that cultural customs make the experience of being an adolescent quite different in various parts of the world.

Moving on to do work in New Guinea, Mead spent some time living with people of the Tchambuli culture. She learned that in their culture, the men were in charge of the household. The women were more active outside the home. This reversal from traditional Western roles again proved her point that culture influences behavior.

anthropologist: A scientist who studies human beings, including their race, environment, and culture.

23

One of her main messages was that we can all benefit from learning about other cultural groups. She believed strongly that patterns of racism, warfare, and other negative behaviors were learned. She felt that people could work together to make the world a better place. As she phrased it, "Never doubt that a small group of thoughtful, committed citizens can change the world."

Getting the Most out of Life

When everything in her life went wrong, Alexandra Hughes Bannister realized that life was too short to waste. She decided to leave England and go off on an adventure.

At the end of 1996, Bannister and five camels set off from Byron Bay on the east coast of Australia. Her goal was to walk around the continent with the camels. She set up a web site so that school students could follow her progress. Alexandra Bannister wasn't the first person to see the places that she visited. But she was the first to make this trip with camels.

racism: Prejudice against a person because of his or her race.

Chapter 2: Introduction

Imagine . . .

that you are set adrift in a small sailboat with no idea of which way to head to get home.

Milton and Joel tied a blindfold tightly over Leila's eyes. Then she heard the sound of one of them jumping down into the small motorboat.

"You can try to confuse me, but I'll still find my way back," Leila said, smiling confidently.

The boy on the pier lifted her, and the boy in the boat caught hold of her.

Leila snatched about wildly, looking for some support. The motorboat bucked and rolled with the motion of the choppy sea.

Her hands found a metal crossbar, and she gripped it. She did not want to be pitched out into the sea.

The twin motors of the *Rancour* came alive. She felt their power as the boat took off from the pier. Then the bow rose as the boat bucked out across the chop of the wind-driven waves.

Still, neither of the boys spoke. They wanted her completely lost for both direction and distance.

Leila's mind slipped back. She had been preparing *Dreamspin*, her sailboat, before they blindfolded her. She had noted the cloudy sky with no sign of the sun. The sea was choppy, and the wind had been gusting.

It was the wind that had made up the boys' mind. It was swinging in from different directions. That would confuse her sense of direction. They continued on for about half an hour, then began to circle before cutting the motors.

Joel took off the blindfold. "Okay, smarty," he said. "Over the side."

Milton had pulled *Dreamspin* alongside, and Leila climbed unsteadily over. The blindfold had made her slightly dizzy.

"Stay in radio contact," Milton said. "We'll come and save you when you are ready to give up."

Rancour's motors roared, and in a few minutes the motorboat was out of sight.

Leila looked around the horizon. Not a sign of land. She smiled and hauled up the mainsail.

They said she could never find her way back to the island without using a compass. She said there were natural ways, and she knew how to use them.

The mainsail filled, and *Dreamspin* keeled over and began chopping into the swells. Leila fixed the helm and slipped down into the small cabin.

"You're first, Peppersalt," she said. She took the homing pigeon from the small cage.

Up on deck, she let it stand freely in her hand. The bird bobbed its head several times. Then it flew up with the sharp, clattering sound a pigeon's wings make when it takes flight.

Leila sat at the helm and watched the bird circle several times. Then it took off like an arrow, and she turned to follow.

She had three pigeons on board. But she only needed to release a second one before she sighted the island ahead.

She dropped the sail as *Dreamspin* slid in beside the pier. Then she secured her boat with a mooring rope before she went back into the cabin.

"*Dreamspin* to *Rancour*," she called on the radio.

"*Rancour* to *Dreamspin*," Milton's voice came back. "Send up a distress flare to show us where you are, and we'll come and rescue you."

"I can't," she said. "You're not allowed to fire distress flares from the pier. . . ."

Chapter 2
The Seas

Why explore the sea? Fishing was the first reason people went to sea. Mussels, oysters, fish, and whales were all important sources of food and supplies for seaside communities. Fishermen followed whales or schools of fish a long way from the shore.

People also went to sea to trade and to wage war. And there was curiosity about distant lands as well as about the sea itself. Explorers saw the oceans as wild and full of mystery, a chance to find excitement. After all, the oceans went further than the eye could see. There had to be something out there. They imagined finding treasure chests overflowing with rubies and pearls. They might see a mermaid combing the seaweed from her hair. Or they might be welcomed home as a hero.

Yet early sailors had plenty to worry about. They believed that the earth was flat, and if ships went too far they might fall off the edge. Ships might get swamped by a huge wave during a storm. They might get lost in a fog. Fog could appear suddenly, creeping silently across the water until it closed around the ship like a cocoon. With fog blocking out the sun and the stars, the captain could easily steer the ship in the wrong direction.

Navigation

The sun and the stars were the first navigational tools of sailors who dared to sail beyond sight of land. At night, the North Star pointed the way. During the day, there were several instruments that relied on the sun. But, of course, the sun had to be shining to use these tools.

The Vikings were early sea explorers. While at sea, Viking adventurer Floki Vilgerdarson released a raven each day for three days. The first raven flew back to the port the ship had left. The second raven came back to the ship. The third raven flew west. Vilgerdarson guessed that the bird was heading for the nearest land mass. Since it hadn't flown in the direction from which they had come, Vilgerdarson followed it and soon arrived in Iceland. This earned him the nickname Raven Floki.

navigation: Sailing accurately from place to place.

Shopping We Will Go

Europeans liked to trade. Silk, tea, and gold, cinnamon, pepper, and other spices were already being traded by land with China, India, and Africa. But there were problems with trade by land. Camel caravans were slow—easy targets for bandits.

Europeans weren't always allowed to travel the entire trade route themselves. That is because it went through territory that belonged to unfriendly rulers. So the Europeans had to rely on foreigners to perform parts of the trade journey. Goods changed hands several times. This increased the cost of the tea or silk before it even reached England or Spain. Creating trade routes on the sea solved this problem.

Sailing West to Reach the East

In 1519, Ferdinand Magellan left Spain on what would be one of the most important voyages ever made. Although he did not survive to return to Spain, Magellan became the first captain to circumnavigate the globe.

With about 250 men and 5 small ships, Magellan began his journey. He sailed west and south through what

circumnavigate: Sail completely around.

is now the Strait of Magellan at the southern tip of South America. Then he sailed across the Pacific Ocean to reach the Spice Islands. Before Magellan's trip, Europeans had always sailed east around Africa's Cape of Good Hope to reach the Spice Islands.

The day they entered the open ocean, the water was calm, so Magellan named it the Pacific Ocean. By this time, they were already running short of food. The penguin and seal meat they had brought from South America had rotted in the heat. Many of the men became ill.

Hunger was not the only problem. Unknown waters, huge waves, whirlpools, and storms threatened the ships. Without Magellan's great skills as a navigator and leader, they would never have reached the Spice Islands. Magellan and some of his men landed on a small island. There they tried to force the native people to become Christians. Magellan was killed. Eventually, 1 ship and 18 men made it back to Spain.

An Englishman, Sir Francis Drake, completed the second circumnavigation of the world in 1577. During the trip, he put a stop to a mutiny led by Thomas Doughty. Doughty was given a hard choice. He could be

Pacific: Peaceful.

mutiny: Refusal to obey authority.

abandoned on an island, taken back to England to face the courts, or put to death. Doughty chose death. His head was lopped off with a sword.

An Experimental Voyage

Would you risk your life to prove a point? In 1947, the Norwegian anthropologist Thor Heyerdahl did just that. He wanted to test his theory that some of the first settlers in Polynesia could have come by sea from South America. He planned to sail with his crew from Peru in South America to Polynesia in the Pacific Islands. He set out with five other Scandinavians on a very unlikely and risky ocean journey. His craft, named the *Kon-Tiki*, was a balsa wood raft. It was built as a replica of the prehistoric South American vessel the settlers would have used. Many in the scientific community thought this voyage was not possible.

Heyerdahl's craft proved seaworthy. Large waves broke over it and the water drained through the raft's deck, while the raft stayed afloat. After 101 days at sea, guided by the winds and ocean currents, the *Kon-Tiki* ended its voyage in Polynesia. Heyerdahl had proven his point and managed to stay alive doing it. He built

replica: An exact copy or reproduction.

several more boats in the 1970s, including the *Ra II*. That boat was constructed of reeds with the help of Aymara Indians from Bolivia. It completed a 4,000-mile transatlantic crossing.

Around the World

Some people risk everything to meet their goals. In 1988, Kay Cottee, an Australian, sailed around the world in a yacht she had built herself. Cottee was the first woman to sail around the world alone and unassisted. It took 189 days.

In 1998, Karen Thorndike became the first American woman to circumnavigate the earth in open ocean. She went around the five great capes of the world—Cape Horn, Cape of Good Hope, Cape Leeuwin, South East Cape, and South West Cape. A cape is a section of land that juts out into open ocean. Whirlpools, enormous waves, and stormy weather are likely to greet any vessel sailing in seas around a cape.

Following a Dream

When Jesse Martin was 14 years old, he told his mother that he wanted to go on an adventure. He dreamed about being the youngest person to sail nonstop around the world, alone and unassisted.

His mother said it was a good idea, but she probably thought he'd forget about it. Jesse kept planning. His aim was to complete a journey of about 27,000 nautical miles (30,000 miles; 50,000 km).

Jesse's mother finally realized that he was serious about making the trip. So she helped him plan it and lent him money to pay for the 33-foot (10-meter) yacht, the *Lionheart*. It took months to organize everything and prepack all of the meals for the trip. At the age of 17, Jesse set sail.

Jesse started his trip from Melbourne, Australia. To circumnavigate the earth, he would have to sail to the antipodal point on the globe. Then he'd have to sail home around the other side of the world. The point opposite to Melbourne is the Azores islands in the North Atlantic Ocean.

Ten Hours of 30-Foot Waves

When a storm hits at sea, there is no place to hide. During the worst storm Jesse faced, he was awake all night keeping his yacht afloat. The storm lasted ten hours. The yacht was thrown around, and the

antipodal point: The point on the globe that is directly opposite to where you are.

mast hit the water five times. Jesse was worried that the mast would snap or the yacht would capsize. But eventually, the wind died down.

Being alone meant Jesse had to fix everything himself. When a bird flew into his generator, Jesse had to replace a blade. He could not help the injured bird, however. It jumped away into the water.

Finally, Jesse arrived home on October 31, 1999. He was only 18, and he'd made it. Jesse says that the next time he sails around the world, he's going to take a few friends with him. He says they will stop for a good time at all of the interesting places they see along the way.

mast: A tall pole, rising from the deck of a vessel, that supports the sails.

Chapter 3: Introduction

> # Imagine . . .
>
> *that you are in a car accident in the hot desert with nothing but sand for miles around.*

SHE SCREAMED. Then there was just a hissing noise.

She was lying on her side, with her knees pulled up near her chin. Something hard was pressing into her shoulder. Her hip hurt.

Slowly, very slowly, she opened her eyes and looked up. He was hanging above her, not moving.

"Dad," she said softly. Then she screamed it: "Dad! Dad!"

But he still did not move.

Robyn jerked and struggled with the buckle of the seat belt.

It was several moments before it sprang open.

"Ow!" she cried as her full weight pressed down on her hip. Then she scrambled to her feet and worked on her dad's buckle. But it was really jammed.

"Dad?" she whispered.

He did not answer. But he was breathing, and she could not see any wounds. He must have been knocked unconscious.

She pulled sleeping bags from the backseat. She packed them where he would fall, then used a knife to cut his seat belt.

When he fell, he did not make a sound. But he was still breathing.

The windshield had popped out when the four-wheel-drive went over. It lay, unbroken, on the red desert sand. Robyn crawled out through the open space.

The hissing sound continued. It was coming from the motor.

Robyn scrambled from the deep hole that had caused the accident. All around was just flat desert sand.

"Oh, please, somebody help us!" she cried,

suddenly frightened.

There was nothing in any direction but the endless desert.

The heat from the sand and the sun began to make her feel ill. She had not even noticed the heat while they had been traveling in the air-conditioned four-wheel-drive.

She put a hand over her head to try to block the heat from above. Then she saw it. Not very far ahead was a shimmering lake. Someone would live near a lake. She would get help there.

Robyn's father opened his eyes. His mind was foggy, and his head hurt. Then he saw where he was.

"Robyn," he cried, struggling through the window. "Robyn!"

Now he remembered. They had been traveling fast when the steering wheel had jerked in his hand. They had hit a deep hole and tipped over.

He climbed from the hole and looked around. He couldn't see Robyn. Then he noticed footprints in the sand. He began to follow them, assuming they would lead him to Robyn.

It was an hour before he saw her—a tiny figure, way ahead.

"Robyn!" he shouted.

She could not hear him. He tried to run, but the heat was too intense.

She was ill and dizzy, but she kept moving. She had to reach the lake.

The lake was hazy now. Sometimes she could not see it at all. Sometimes she was not sure exactly where it was. She did not even realize that she had begun walking in a circle. But the lake stayed ahead.

Her father saw the circle she was making, and moved toward her. He saw her stumble, then fall.

"Robyn!" he cried. He fell to his knees beside her, covering her with his shadow.

"I have to reach the lake," she said.

Now that he was with her, she forgot that he needed help. All she wanted was to reach the lake so she could crawl into the water away from the heat.

"We have to get back to the car," he said. "There's water there, and shade."

He lifted her to her feet. "You should never have left it."

"But I want to reach the lake!" she cried, struggling to break away from him.

"There is no lake," he said.

She looked for it. But it had gone. "It was . . . somewhere," she said.

"It was just a mirage. The heat shimmering on the sand made it look like a lake," he told her. "We have to get back to the car. Someone will come along in the next day or two. We've got plenty of food and water."

She tried to pull away from him. She wanted to go to the lake. . . .

Chapter 3
The Deserts

"WATER! WATER . . ." The actor comes toward the camera, clutching at his throat, begging to be saved from the parched sands of the desert. Dramatic, isn't it? Yet the reality in many deserts is even tougher. Deserts are places without regular rainfall. Nothing people do can bring rain to the desert. For an explorer, the desert is the harsh side of nature. It can be enough to make explorers ask why they do what they do.

What's in a Desert?

Are there always sand and camels? No. Deserts aren't all the same. Many provide a home for a variety of plants and animals. Others can be like the deserts you see in the movies—endless hot, dry, sand hills.

Some desert dwellers in the Gobi Desert believe that whirlwinds of dust are spirits that use the dust and sand to cover their naked bodies. The local people believe you can tell whether the spirit is male or female depending on how the

parched: Without any moisture, dry.

dust whirls. They also believe that there is an evil spirit in the form of a black eagle. It calls out to travelers for help, then loses them in the desert.

Crossing a Continent

Robert Burke, a man with a bit of a rebellious streak, was a country policeman in southern Australia. He often got lost in the sparsely settled areas of Australia known as the bush. But he probably didn't mention that when he applied to lead an expedition into the unknown north of Australia. William Wills, a surveyor, was appointed second in command.

The expedition plan was to cross the continent from south to north from, sea to sea. The goal was to establish an overland telegraph route to northern Australia. They left Melbourne in August 1860. The group included 3 scientists, 14 assistants, 27 camels, and several horse-drawn wagons carrying 21 tons of supplies.

Still on the Move

As the expedition reached its first camp, Burke decided it would be faster to split up. So Burke and Wills, 6 other men,

rebellious:
Acting against
authority.

15 horses, and 16 camels went ahead. It was October. They headed north. One man was sent back to get more supplies and meet them later at Cooper's Creek, the second camp.

Burke's party reached Cooper's Creek on November 11. They set up camp but were driven out by a plague of rats. The next camp was better, and they waited for supplies to arrive. It was still 1,500 miles (2,500 km) to their northern goal and back. Burke was eager to get going, so he split the group again. He took Wills, King, and Gray north on December 16. Burke wanted to reach the northern coast. They expected to be gone for three months. The others stayed at Cooper's Creek to wait for the supplies.

To Almost See the Sea

The four men set a good pace. Soon they reached the tropics, but they hadn't counted on the wet

season. The rain poured down on their heads, and the camels slipped in the mud. Burke and Wills covered the last 30 miles (50 km) on foot. Eventually, they came to a swamp. The water in the creeks was salty, and the tides made the water rise and fall. Thick clumps of tree roots blocked their way. But they knew that the salty tidal water meant the sea was very close. It was February 10, 1861. They had made it.

There was no time to waste. Burke and Wills returned to Gray and King. They had to hurry back south to Cooper's Creek before they ran out of food. The tropical rain made the going hard. Then there was the frying heat of the desert in the middle of summer. They were all tired and weak from lack of food. By April they were forced to kill a horse for food. But it was too late for Gray. On April 17, he died from exhaustion. They were only 70 miles (110 km) from Cooper's Creek.

Waiting and Waiting

Back at Cooper's Creek, there was confusion. The supplies that should have arrived six months before never did. There had been no word from Burke. There was nothing to do but shoot the rats and wait. Because there were no fresh fruits or vegetables, the men started to develop scurvy. It hurt to chew. They waited for Burke and

scurvy: A disease caused by lack of vitamin C. It can affect the gums and loosen teeth.

the others until April 21. Then, at 10:30 that morning, they left Cooper's Creek.

At sunrise on April 21, Burke, Wills, and King set off for Cooper's Creek. They traveled all day, and they finally limped into camp at 7:30 P.M. To their horror, they read the departure date carved into a tree. After months of waiting, the two groups had missed each other by only nine hours.

Burke, Wills, and King found the supplies left by the others. But it was too late to be of much good. They were already so weak that they needed fresh food, including fruit and vegetables, to regain their strength. The disappointment they felt must have been overwhelming. At the beginning of July, Wills died, followed soon after by Burke. King, cared for by a local tribe, was eventually found by a rescue team.

Even though Burke and Wills died, they had achieved their goal—to cross the Australian continent. They had traveled 1,500 miles (2,500 km) in 6 months.

Death by Salt

In 1893, Sven Hedin from Sweden traveled to the Taklimakan Desert in China. He wanted to explore areas that had not yet been recorded on the map of the world. The desert he found was so flat and featureless that there were no landmarks with which to take his bearings. When his team ran out of water, two assistants drank camel urine. They died bloated with salt. Since camels are good at retaining water in their bodies, their urine has a very high salt and toxin content. The men should have drunk their own urine.

Daughter of the Desert

In 1899, Gertrude Bell made her first archaeological expedition into the desert areas of the Middle East. For the next 15 years, she traveled widely throughout the deserts of the region. The Arabs called her "Daughter of the Desert."

She was fascinated by the history and the people.

toxin: A poisonous substance.

archaeological: About the study of past cultures through the objects they left behind.

Bell made the effort to learn to speak Persian and Arabic. So she was able to travel more easily and didn't need as many guides as other Westerners. Many of the archaeological sites Bell recorded have eroded or completely disappeared. The records she made are the only detailed facts that exist about certain sites.

Most women at that time led very restricted lives. But Bell was braving the desert with local male guides as her companions. Heat and lack of water weren't the only natural dangers that she had to overcome. Storms could make it impossible for people or animals to move. During a desert storm, clouds often roll across the sky, blocking out the sun and daylight. Fierce winds hurl stones and choking sands everywhere.

On one trip, the team was crossing a plain of hard mud when it started to rain heavily. Almost immediately the rain stopped, but the ground had become a slimy, yellow mud bath. The horses struggled to drag their feet through the mess. In a serious rainstorm, they would have been completely stuck in the mud. Then they would have had to wait hours until the earth dried out.

eroded: Been worn away by the action of wind, rain, or glacial ice.

Risk Is the Salt and Sugar of Life

Freya Stark learned the languages of the Middle East. Then, in 1927, she set out to explore areas of Iran that no other Westerner had ever seen. She traveled widely in southern Arabia and later retraced the footsteps of Alexander the Great. Second-best and safest was never good enough for Stark. She was always slipping into areas that the British government stated were off limits because they were too dangerous. According to Stark, the biggest problem with modern life is that it encourages us to take the easy way. What do you think? Are the spirit of adventure and the courage to push the limits of what can be achieved gone?

Chapter 4: Introduction

> # Imagine . . .
>
> *that you and your brother have set off to climb a dangerous mountain.*

"I'LL CLIMB old Lottle one day soon," Alistair said. "Just as soon as I have all of the climbing gear I need. I'll bring you children back a stone from the peak."

"We are not children!" Meg snapped.

"Don't get so upset, cousin," Alistair laughed as he rode away.

"He's such a big show-off!" Angus cried. "Why is he always teasing and treating us like children?"

Meg looked up at Mt. Lottle. It was a small mountain. It did not rise even a thousand feet. But it was difficult to climb, and many people came to Scotland just to try.

"We could climb it," Meg said to her younger brother. "That would keep cousin Alistair quiet."

"Let's!" Angus said.

They packed lunches after breakfast and put them in plastic bags so they would not need a backpack.

Their mother was already at work in her craft shop when they were ready to leave.

"We're going up to Mt. Lottle," Meg said. "We've packed lunches."

"Is Alistair going with you?" her mother asked.

"I haven't seen him," Meg said.

They told their father they were going as they passed him. He was plowing the side field.

Mt. Lottle was about a mile beyond their small farm. It rose

quickly, as if it had been pushed straight up out of the ground, ready-made. It was a very steep climb, but Meg and Angus had been climbing among rocks all of their lives.

"We'll climb it easily," Angus said.

They were nearly halfway to the top when they stopped for lunch on a wide ledge.

They did not stop for long. Angus was soon climbing the next steep rock face.

"Lean down and help!" Meg called when he was up. "My foot keeps slipping."

Angus leaned down and helped her up the rock face.

The next rock face was higher, and neither of them could get a toehold.

"I'll crouch down, and you get on my back," Angus said.

Using his back, Meg was able to reach the ledge above and roll herself onto it. Then she leaned down and hauled Angus up.

But that was as high as they could go. The next rock face was too high, even when Meg climbed onto Angus's back.

"We need something to hammer into the rock," Angus said.

"We'll have to go back and try another way," Meg said. She lay down and looked over the edge. "It's a long way back to the ledge," she said.

Angus got down and looked, too. "We need a rope," he said. "If one of us slipped . . ."

He did not finish. He did not need to. They both knew stories of climbers who had rolled off a ledge. Their ropes had snapped or been lost, and the climbers had plunged to their death. And he and Meg did not even have a rope.

They were shivering with cold as night fell. In the darkness below they could see spotlights that moved across the fields.

"They're searching for us," Angus said. "I wish we had a flare or a signal lamp."

"I wish we had sleeping bags or thermal blankets," Meg answered.

By the next morning, they were both so stiff with cold that they found it hard to move. But they knew they had to signal. People would be scanning Mt. Lottle with binoculars. They always did that when anyone was lost.

They used the plastic bags to wave.

Two hours later, James MacGregor hauled himself up onto the ledge beside them. He was a strong man and one of the best climbers in the district.

He was angry, and they could not meet his eyes. He shook his head and handed them a bottle of water.

"Take a swig of that," he said. Then he got a spike from his belt and drove it deep into the rock. Driving it in seemed to take the anger from him.

"You are safe now," he said, "and you've climbed well. But you're lucky to be here to tell about it. . . ."

Chapter 4

The Mountains

IN SPITE OF THE OBVIOUS DANGERS, there are
many adventurers who want to climb mountains.
Many of them feel the higher the better. That is
why climbing Mt. Everest, the world's highest
mountain, holds such fascination for so many. For
years, Everest has been the scene of triumph for
some and death for others.

Climbing a mountain always requires a strategy.
Because of the high risk, every expedition to climb
Everest takes detailed and careful planning.

Air Problems

What are some of the risks of climbing Mt.
Everest? The main risk is lack of oxygen. The
higher you climb, the less oxygen there is in the
air. Less oxygen makes it harder to breathe and
function. Although bottles of oxygen help
climbers, they are not as reliable or user-friendly
as the air around us.

Another risk is that climbers can suffer from
altitude sickness. Any area above 25,000 feet

(7,600 meters) is called the death zone. Mt. Everest is 29,028 feet (8,849 meters) high. Every climber trying to make it to the top enters the death zone. There climbers can suffer headaches, loss of appetite, and extreme tiredness. This might not sound too serious. But in dangerous situations, such as climbing a mountain, you need all of your energy and concentration.

If a climber spends too long in the death zone, there can be serious consequences. Lungs can fill with fluid, making it impossible to breathe. Blood circulation can speed up, causing the brain to swell. Once this starts to happen, death can occur within a few hours.

First Conquest of Mt. Everest

"We didn't know if it was humanly possible to reach the top of Mt. Everest. And even using oxygen as we were, if we did get to the top, we weren't at all sure whether we wouldn't drop dead. . . ." These are the words of Sir Edmund Hillary of New Zealand. He is describing his fears before his historic climb in 1953.

Summit: The highest point.

Hillary joined a British expedition to climb Everest. Before and after that, many people who failed to reach the summit died or were severely injured. Avalanches, violent storms, high altitude, and treacherous terrain have all taken their toll on climbers. Some climbers have been lost on the frigid slopes. Others have later endured amputation due to frostbite.

A Sherpa guide

The Sherpas are a group of people living mostly in the Himalayan mountain range of Nepal. They act as guides on many Everest expeditions. In 1922, seven Sherpas died in an avalanche on the mountain. Since that time, one-third of Everest's victims have been Sherpas. So it was particularly fitting that Tenzing Norgay, a Sherpa, was with Sir Edmund Hillary on May 29, 1953. On that day, the two men shared the triumph of being the first humans to reach the summit of Mt. Everest—the highest point on Earth.

Getting the Gear up the Mountain

The development of bottled oxygen made it easier to climb and stay on the mountain longer. But it also meant that expeditions needed to employ more Sherpas to carry the oxygen. On Hillary's expedition, there were 36 Sherpas helping to carry supplies and equipment. Equipment alone, however, is not enough to ensure success. It still takes an amazing mix of planning, effort, experience, and luck to get to the summit.

The Elements Still Rule the Mountains

Storms can appear suddenly in the Himalayas. Wind and cold are killers on the high peaks. When it is hard to see, a climber can take a wrong turn. This can mean a fall off the side of a cliff thousands of feet high. Falling rocks and avalanches are a constant threat and can happen without warning.

In 1996, Rob Hall, an experienced professional guide, led a group of climbers on an Everest expedition. They reached Camp 4 at 26,000 feet (7,927 meters). They waited there for good weather before attempting to climb to the summit.

It had already been an exhausting climb. Some members developed hacking coughs. Others couldn't sleep at night and felt nauseous whenever they tried to eat. Yet everyone

nauseous: Sick to one's stomach.

was excited and impatient to start the final leg of the climb. Before they left, Hall told the climbers how important it was that they stay close together. Then, if anything went wrong, they could help each other.

Sticking Together

The faster climbers didn't like waiting for the others. They got cold and grumpy. As they got higher, there were delays because several other expeditions were trying to climb at the same time. It was a traffic jam in the death zone. Half of Hall's team turned back, exhausted and worried about running out of oxygen. They returned to Camp 4.

There were technical problems, too. Safety ropes needed to be set up on some parts of the climb. They had been told that the ropes were already there. But they weren't. Bad weather prevented the Sherpas from going ahead of the group to check everything. So the ropes had to be set up very quickly. More delays.

Time and oxygen were running out. When one member of the team, American writer Jon Krakauer, made it to the top, he was too tired to be excited. He was also worried about making the climb down with an oxygen supply that was

running low. As he turned to start the downward trek, he noticed clouds gathering. He didn't realize that they were storm clouds. One by one, the remaining climbers made it to Everest's summit as the storm drew closer.

Fifteen minutes after leaving the summit, Krakauer came to a steep rock face known as the Hillary Step. He had to wait while another team of climbers came up before he could climb down. While he was waiting, Andy Harris, one of the guides, joined him. Krakauer asked Harris to close the valves to his oxygen tank to save the small amount he had left. But Harris's mind was unclear because of the altitude, and he opened the valves instead of closing them. Within ten minutes, all of Krakauer's oxygen was gone.

Should You Always Trust Equipment?

At the first storage point for oxygen tanks on the way down, Harris checked the oxygen tanks. He said they were empty. Everyone was shocked but assumed he was right. People who reached the storage point later discovered that Harris had made a mistake. The oxygen gauge he used to check the tanks wasn't working. But because his brain was working slowly at that altitude, he didn't question his equipment. Mistakes like this were piling up.

The storm was getting really serious. The wind roared between the thunder and lightning. Snow filled the air, stinging the climbers' faces. With the windchill factor, the temperature was −100°F (−73°C).

There were several radios in the group, but not all of them were working because of the freezing temperatures. Since the group wasn't sticking together, some individuals were completely out of touch with the others.

Who Will Help?

It became obvious to those who had made it back to Camp 4 that a rescue party was needed. But there were more problems. Two Sherpas had carbon monoxide poisoning from cooking in a tent that wasn't properly ventilated. They were vomiting blood and were too sick to help anyone. Others, who had

windchill factor: The temperature felt on exposed skin, which is the actual temperature plus the chilling effect of the wind.

made it back from the summit, were exhausted from their climb.

By the next morning, it was clear that the situation was becoming disastrous. The wind was still strong, and it was cold. Hall and Doug Hansen, another climber, were stuck near the summit. Harris had gone back to help them. All three died before the weather cleared enough for anyone to get to them. Krakauer recalled that the tears in his eyes froze his eyelids shut.

Eventually Anatoli Boukreev, one of the guides, found a group of lost team members. Yasuko Namba, a Japanese climber, and Beck Weathers, an American, were barely alive. Three inches (8 cm) of ice had to be chipped off their faces. Boukreev had to make a decision—should he help two people who would probably die soon anyway? The rest of the team was sick and exhausted. The extra pressure of looking after these two could end in a bigger disaster. Finally, the decision was made to try to save the team members who had the best chance. Yasuko Namba and Beck Weathers were left in the snow to die.

A Miracle at Last

In the afternoon, someone with a funny-looking stiff walk, a missing glove, and vicious frostbite walked into Camp 4. It was Weathers—after being in a coma for 12 hours. He was put into two sleeping bags with hot water bottles and an oxygen mask. No one expected him to live through the night. He did. He was taken to lower ground and evacuated by rescue helicopter.

The remainder of the team started the descent from Camp 4. Their run of bad luck was not over. A big stone whizzed down from further up the mountain. It hit one of the Sherpas on the back of the head and knocked him unconscious.

Four of the original team were dead. Emotions and enthusiasm played a part in the disaster. Once climbers get so close to realizing their dream, it is hard to turn around because time is running out. Climbing Mt. Everest means taking a risk. Perhaps that's why people want to try it for themselves.

Weathers returned to his home in Texas. The frostbite was so severe that his right arm had to be amputated below the elbow. Four fingers and the thumb were removed from his left hand, and his nose was amputated and reconstructed. It was the price he paid for seeing what has been called the "best view in the world."

amputated: Removed by surgery.

Caring for the Mountain

Imagine how much litter must be on Mt. Everest from the almost 1,000 people who have climbed it.

In 1988, an Australian Everest expedition was the first team to take all of its trash back down the mountain. Hopefully, this example will be followed by all future climbers.

The Start to a New Adventure

Many modern cliff-hangers began their careers at an indoor climbing center. Many still practice there when they can't be in the great outdoors.

Indoor climbing centers have handholds and footholds on the walls. A safety rope is attached to the climber, the ceiling, and the climber's partner. The partner adjusts the rope as the climber needs it. That way, the climber can take risks and try difficult moves without the danger of crashing to the ground.

Chapter 5: Introduction

Imagine . . .

*that you are in a kayak off
Greenland exploring the wildlife.*

"SEAL HO!" Dad shouted from ahead and plunged his paddle into the sea.

Mom and I snatched up our paddles and pushed away from the side of the iceberg. Both of us were paddling hard. But the double sea kayak was slower than the single one that Dad was in.

"There it is, Mom!" I shouted as the snout of a seal broke the surface ahead of Dad.

Mom swapped her paddle for her camera, and I swung our kayak toward the seal. Dad was already filming. While Mom filmed Dad filming the seal, I kept the kayak moving in a wide circle.

Mom and Dad make documentaries for television. You've probably seen some of them. Have you ever wondered how you could see the person doing the filming? In our documentaries, it is always Mom or Dad filming with a second camera.

This documentary is to be called *The Seals off Greenland*. If you ever watch it, you'll know who was doing the filming. You'll also know who was doing all of the hard paddling. Me.

Everyone said I was too young to come on such a dangerous expedition. Everyone except Mom and Dad. They said ten years old was old enough. And they were right.

"Go back closer to the iceberg, Ronnie," Mom called. "I might be able to get a shot of Dad reflected in the ice."

I swung our kayak around, and Mom turned her camera toward the iceberg.

Then she screamed a warning.

But it was too late. A huge chunk of ice had split away from near the top of the iceberg.

I dug the paddle in and hauled. The bow of our kayak began to swing, but the ice fell too quickly. It crashed down beside us. It slit the hull and created a huge wave that slapped against the iceberg. Then the wave came back and flipped our kayak over.

I was pitched out into the sea. Even my life jacket could not stop me from going underwater. The sea swirled around us like a miniature storm.

"Dad," I choked as I came to the surface.

Mom had not been able to get free. She was trapped under the overturned kayak.

I was only a few paddles away, and I reached the boat before Dad did. But I could not dive under because of my life jacket.

Dad reached down and pulled me onto his boat. "Lie across and try to lift!"

We heaved, and the double kayak came up enough for Mom's head to be free. She was coughing and choking.

Dad swung his other arm over and locked it into the collar of her life jacket.

"Kick yourself free!" Dad cried.

I don't think Mom could hear him, but she was kicking anyway and suddenly slid out. I let the kayak go then and helped Dad drag her over the top of our boat.

"She's drowned!" I screamed.

A great whoosh of vomit and water came out of Mom's mouth into the sea.

"I'm not!" she cried.

The swirling sea had already died down. The water was smooth again. But we were in mortal danger. Mom was so chilled by the water that she could die from the cold.

At least we were all alive. But we needed to get warm fast.

Dad reached into the sea and snatched one of the paddles floating beside the overturned kayak.

"Paddle!" he shouted and pointed toward a small, rocky island.

Sitting on the kayak as though it was a horse, I paddled with all my strength. My whole body was warm again by the time we reached the rock.

There was a small cave, and we carried Mom into it. Then I ran back to Dad's kayak and got all of the sleeping bags.

Mom was going to be all right . . . for now.

Dad pointed to the water marks on the cave walls.

"This cave is underwater at high tide," he said. "We're going to have to find shelter somewhere else. Quickly. . . ."

Chapter 5
The Poles

A MAGNETIC FORCE runs through the center of the earth along a north-south line called an axis. The Poles are the points at the ends of the axis.

Earth spins on the axis from west to east once every 24 hours. That is why we see the sun rising in the east and setting in the west every day. It is the spin that gives us night and day.

Are Both Poles the Same?

The North Pole is in water that is covered by ice. The ice is surrounded by land. The North Pole is actually a point in the middle of the region called the Arctic Circle. The Arctic Circle includes Greenland and the most northern parts of Canada, Alaska, Scandinavia, and Russia. The South Pole is in the middle of land that is surrounded by water. This land mass is called Antarctica.

Even today, exploration in the Arctic is still a huge challenge. Much of the Arctic region is made up of water. The waves and tides move the surface ice around so much that the whole area is unpredictable. Also, there are giant icebergs moving in the water. Without warning, huge pieces can fall off the icebergs. These can easily crush a boat, dumping the survivors into the Arctic's frigid waters.

Extreme Conditions

In the 1920s, Gino Watkins, a 23-year-old student from England, made his first trip to Greenland in the Arctic Circle. He was popular with his team, and he soon formed close friendships with some of the local people. A hunter called Ippa Kaj taught Watkins how to build a small boat like the ones the Inuits use for traveling and hunting. Watkins quickly realized the benefits of the sea kayak. It would be easier to explore in such a small boat. There would be less chance of getting locked in by moving ice.

In 1931, Watkins returned to explore the rugged east coast of Greenland by ship and kayak. During that trip, Watkins lifted his kayak onto the ice so that he could go for a walk. But he didn't secure it properly. The kayak slipped into the water and started to float

Inuits: Eskimo people.

away. Watkins jumped into the water and swam after the kayak. But the kayak was too far away. Watkins drowned in the freezing water before he could reach the boat. In 1986, a group of Australians completed Gino Watkins's unfinished kayak trip around the coast of Greenland.

Life Skills

In 1845, Sir John Robert Franklin set off by ship on an expedition to the Arctic. He was looking for a sea route that would link the Atlantic and Pacific Oceans. On board the ship were 129 men and enough food for 3 years. They thought they had everything they needed with them. Yet none of them ever returned. When they were forced to abandon the ice-locked ship, they didn't have enough clothes to keep them warm. They only had regulation navy uniforms with extra-warm underwear. They didn't have enough vegetables to eat. They soon got so sick that their appearance scared away the Inuits they met. The Inuits were the only people who could have helped them.

regulation: official.

Early Arctic explorers soon realized that they could increase their chances of survival by learning from the local people. They ate the local diet. They often relied on Inuit guides. They wore the same clothes as the native people, made out of seal skin and polar bear fur. The clothing was half the weight of the clothing they usually wore. The explorers also learned to use dogs called huskies to pull their sleds.

A Warm Spot in a Storm

Being caught in an Arctic storm without shelter is a death sentence. Temperatures plummet to −58°F (−50°C), and wind cuts through clothes. Swirling snow makes it impossible to know which direction to follow. The wind can get so strong it is impossible to walk. If you sit down and wait for the storm to end, you'll freeze to death. Even if the wind is not quite strong enough to prevent walking, you can get lost. Not very good options, are they?

The Inuits have taught foreign explorers how to build igloos out of snow bricks. Explorers caught in bad weather can build an igloo in less than two hours. Many explorers have relied on that skill of building a shelter to stay alive.

Inuit hunter Ippa Kaj had just shot a bear when a storm hit very suddenly. He cut a hole in the skin of the bear and hid in the guts to keep warm. Ippa Kaj was inside the animal's body for two days. Imagine how strange that must have felt. Would you do that to survive?

First to the Pole

In 1908, Robert Peary, an American, prepared to set out on his final attempt to reach the North Pole. By this time, Peary had already spent almost 20 years exploring the unforgiving Arctic region. There he had suffered enormous hardships, including the loss of most of his toes to frostbite. Twice before, he had tried to reach the North Pole. But each time he was forced back by the brutal Arctic climate. Now 52 years old, Peary was as determined as ever to reach his goal.

This was to be his final expedition. Peary took 4 Eskimo dogsledders, 40 sled dogs, and 4 sleds loaded with food and scientific equipment. He was also accompanied by his chief assistant, Matthew Henson. Henson was an African American who had gone with Peary on all of his Arctic expeditions. This time the expedition was a success. On April 6, 1909, Peary announced that he had become the first person to reach the North Pole. But was it true?

No Cheers for Peary

There was very little excitement when the news broke that Robert Peary had reached the North Pole. Only one week earlier, another American explorer had claimed to have reached the North Pole a year before Peary. His name was Frederick Cook. After a lengthy investigation, Cook could not prove his claim. Years later, he was sent to prison for mail fraud.

But Peary had other doubters. They claimed that Peary had miscalculated his location and missed the Pole by 30 to 60 miles. For 80 years, the arguments continued. Finally, in 1989, a study by the National Geographic Society concluded that Peary had told the truth. He was indeed the first person to reach the North Pole.

Explorers, but Not the First

Many explorers who were hailed as the first to do something were simply the first to claim to be first. The first explorers of the Arctic region

miscalculated:
Incorrectly
figured out.

were not the first people there. The Inuits have been living in the Arctic region for thousands of years. However, the people who come from all over the world to explore the Arctic region have achieved great things. And they have shown amazing bravery. Explorers have also helped to introduce other cultures to the rest of the world. For example, by bringing the kayak to England, Gino Watkins acquainted westerners with a part of Inuit life.

From the North to the South

Many of the first explorers in Antarctica had already been to the Arctic Circle. Unlike the Arctic, there were no native people in Antarctica. So explorers relied on the survival skills they had learned from the Inuits, such as using huskies. Roald Amundsen from Norway and Robert Scott from England both wanted to be the first to reach the South Pole. It became a race between the two men and their teams.

Man's Best Friend

In 1911, Amundsen took 118 huskies and 4 men to the Antarctic. Scott had 33 men, 33 dogs, 17 ponies, and 2 motorized sleds. The engines gave out quickly in the freezing conditions. The ponies all died. Only the dogs coped. After a terrible struggle, Scott and his party reached the South Pole. Imagine their disappointment when they found that the Norwegians had beaten them to it. On the return trip, cold, storms, and a lack of supplies were too much. Scott and his fellow explorers all died from a mixture of cold, hunger, and exhaustion.

When Amundsen returned, he had achieved his goal, and he and his four-man team were all healthy. But there were only 11 dogs left—the expedition party had used the rest as food.

During the 1990s, there was a debate about allowing animals that are not native to Antarctica on the continent. There was a concern that non-native animals could spread diseases to the native seals and birds. According to Dr. Phillip Law who ran Australia's Antarctica territories for almost 20 years, huskies had never caused a problem. He felt that they were no threat to the environment. However, huskies are now banned from Antarctica.

Can Anything Else Go Wrong?

Yes, it can! One Antarctica explorer was collecting urine samples to see how his body was coping. It ended in

debate: verbal argument.

disaster. The glass container came in contact with his skin. The freezing air temperature caused the glass to stick. When he pulled the glass away, his skin came with it. That was the end of his expedition for the year.

Some people have gone mad from isolation or lack of food. Cold, injuries, sunburn, frostbite, and exhaustion all take their toll on the body. Can you imagine risking your life struggling through the snow and wind day after day?

So Why Go?

Dr. Phillip Law explored over 1,800 miles of Antarctic coastline. He says that there is a big difference between discovery and exploration. Discovery means seeing or reaching some point. Exploration is about getting information to create a map of the area, getting samples of rocks or plants, and learning something. Since Antarctica is frozen, many of the earth's secrets are safely held there. Exploration in Antarctica is an amazing chance to learn about millions of years of evolution.

On the other hand, exploration can be as much about testing your own personality as it is about exploring the world.

Some people are just interested in breaking a

world record. "Sometimes I think someone will try crawling to the South Pole on their hands and knees just to get into the record books," says Law. Others, however, may want to prove themselves or learn how much the human body can endure. Still others want to enjoy a challenge and escape from their regular lives.

What Antarctic Adventures Are Left?

No one has managed to walk across Antarctica yet. Many have tried, including American Helen Thayer. Thayer was injured when a violent wind picked up her 257-pound (117-kg) supply sled and slammed it into her leg. Sixty-year-old Thayer was no beginner. She had been the first woman to complete a solo trek to the magnetic north pole in 1988 at the age of 50.

Boerge Ousland from Norway skied across Antarctica. When the wind was right, he used a sail to increase his speed.

Antarctica is a wilderness that remains to be explored. There are still mountains and glaciers to be climbed, scientific discoveries to be made, and treks to be done. Could you be a polar explorer?

Chapter 6: Introduction

Imagine . . .

that you and your family lived in a spaceship where you were weightless.

"MOM! MOM! The baby's escaped again!"

"Oh, no!" Mom said. "Who took the lid off his crib?"

"I'll get the hook," Fran said.

"No! I want to hook him if he's on the ceiling!" Brad said. "It's my turn!"

"Just find him first," Mom said.

"Billy! Billy!" Fran called as she ran off through the house.

"When are you going to put G-boots on him, Mom?" Brad asked.

"You can't put G-boots on a baby," Mom

said as she went along the hall to the nursery.

She checked the crib. The lid was open, and there was no sign of Billy.

"I'm glad we don't have windows that open," she said. "Otherwise, we'd never see him again."

Brad went to get the hook from under the crib. But it was already gone.

"Fran's taken the hook!" he cried. "It's my turn!"

"Just find Billy!" Mom said. "That's the important thing."

Mom went to look in her bedroom. Dad was asleep there. He had been on observation duty.

Mom shook him gently. "Billy's gone again," she said.

Dad grunted and turned the cover back. He floated from the bed and pulled himself down to put on his G-boots so he could stand. "He was in his crib when I came off duty," he said.

"I've found him! I've found him!" Fran called. "He's in the schoolroom!"

Billy used his tiny fingers to pull himself along the ceiling.

"I can't reach him!" Fran called. She held the hook in the very tips of her fingers and jumped. But she was not tall enough to reach her baby brother.

Billy gurgled with laughter. Tiny bubbles of spit came from his mouth and floated in front of his face. He tried to reach them with his hands, and he gurgled some more.

"The sooner he's old enough for G-boots the better," Dad said. He lifted Fran up so she could reach Billy with the hook.

Fran got the hook around the baby and pulled him down.

"I don't know how he gets the top of his crib off," Mom said as they walked to the nursery. "You two were much older before you began escaping."

Dad set the baby in the air above his crib while he changed him.

Mom checked the top of the crib. "Tie it with a ribbon as well as locking it," she said. She looked at the time. "I'm on observation duty in 20 minutes. I'll go and change."

She was nearly out the door when she remembered. "One of you catch all of Billy's spit bubbles," she reminded them.

Fran was looking out the window at the green-blue ball way in the distance.

"Are we going back to Earth for our vacation this year, Dad?" she asked.

"Yep," he said as he put Billy back in his crib and locked it.

"I wouldn't want to live on Earth all the time," Brad said. "I always feel so heavy when we're there."

"It's going to be a surprise for Billy," Dad said. "He won't be able to float his way up to the ceiling there."

"Swimming is the only good thing on Earth," Fran said. "It's the only time I feel normal when I'm there. The rest of the time gravity just makes me feel stuck."

She got a tissue. Then she took off her

G-boots and gave a little jump. Up near the ceiling she chased and caught all of Billy's spit bubbles in the tissue. Then she pushed off the ceiling to go back to the floor.

"I'm glad you and Mom are space scientists," she said. "I'd much rather live here in space than in an Earth house."

She put her G-boots back on. Their magnetic soles gripped the floor just enough to hold her so she didn't float when she walked. She carried the tissue over to the wastebasket. . . .

Chapter 6
Air and Space

If PEOPLE were supposed to fly, they would have been born with wings . . .

For thousands of years, humans have watched in awe as birds soared above them. Gradually, more individuals dreamed of flying. There had to be a way for us to attach feathers and wings and fly, too, didn't there? Wings were made. But takeoff was a problem. People thought that if they could get high enough on a cliff to catch the air currents, they could fly.

Several people died when they jumped, flapped their newly made wings, and crashed to the earth. Then there was a breakthrough. What if wings were solidly attached?

In 1902, Wilbur and Orville Wright built and tested a winged glider. It stayed airborne for 620 feet (189 meters). They were thrilled. By 1903, the brothers had a motor for the glider. They'd made the first airplane. Now only the sky was the limit.

But these early planes had a few limitations. The engines were small and unreliable. The cockpit, where the pilot sat, was open. Refueling had to be done regularly, and bad weather made flying very dangerous.

Amelia Earhart

By 1937, American Amelia Earhart was one of the first female pilots willing to try long-distance flying. On May 21, she left California in an attempt to be the first woman to fly around the world. It was going to be a record-breaking trip. During the trip, she became the first person to fly from the Red Sea to India. Along the way, there were many stops to refuel and make repairs to equipment. Bad weather and fatigue were regular problems. Even before the trip, Earhart thought it would be her last big flight. "I mean to give up long-distance 'stunt' flying," she said.

In Indonesia, Earhart was gripped with dysentery. Everyone who saw her after that said she looked tired and ill. Repairs were made at Darwin, Australia, and then Earhart made the short flight to New Guinea. After that there were 7,000 miles (12,000 km) to go—over the Pacific. The plane carried 1,000 gallons (4,546 liters) of fuel, allowing for about 20 hours of flying. About seven hours after takeoff, Earhart radioed a position

dysentery: An intestinal illness.

report. The head wind was increasing. No one knows if Earhart heard the radio report that went out to her. About 20 hours after takeoff, Earhart made radio contact with the U.S. Coast Guard. She was looking for Howland Island where she was expected to land. But she couldn't see land. Fuel was running low.

On July 2, 1937, after flying 22,000 miles (36,667 km), Earhart and her navigator, Fred Noonan, disappeared. Even today, no one knows what happened.

Amelia Earhart was prepared to take risks. She pushed herself to the limit to achieve new heights in aviation. She wrote a poem and gave it to a friend. The first line reads, "Courage is the price that Life exacts for granting peace."

Helicopter Heaven

In the early 1980s, Australian Dick Smith sold his successful electronics business in order to take up full-time adventuring. He hated being stuck in the office. "I love adventure," he said. Smith decided to fly the full circle of the globe in a helicopter, starting in Texas.

On the first day, Smith flew around the Statue of Liberty. The reality of the bird's-eye view of the earth was already living up to the dream.

As he flew north across Canada, the helicopter was buffeted by gale-force winds. Smith was forced to make an unscheduled stop on a small island in the Arctic Circle. He spent the night shivering in his sleeping bag. He didn't sleep much, thanks to persistent mosquitoes, rumbling icebergs, and barking dogs. Later, he found out that the barking came from seals.

In 1983, Smith became the first person to fly a helicopter around the world. It took 319 hours and 36 minutes of flying time to complete the trip of 39,000 miles (65,000 km). Smith also flies hot-air balloons. He made several attempts to take his balloon from New Zealand to Australia—against the prevailing winds. Finally, in February 2000, after a two-day flight, he achieved that goal, too.

National Pride

The cost of space travel is enormous. So it takes a nation to want to reach the skies rather than just a few brave individuals. While an individual may be most interested in the adventure and achievement, the government can have more complicated motives. For the United States

> buffeted:
> Blown around
> by, battered.

and the former Soviet Union, being first in the space race was a matter of national pride. Whose flag would claim the first landing on the moon?

Soviets First in Space

On the morning of April 12, 1961, cosmonaut Yuri Gagarin woke up after a good night's sleep. People were surprised that he could sleep through the night before his attempt to be the first person in space. Gagarin's response was matter-of-fact. "Would it be right to take off if I was not rested? It was my duty to sleep, so I slept."

Gagarin waited for liftoff. At liftoff, he felt five times heavier than his regular weight. In space, he maneuvered his body and the instruments despite the weightlessness. The effects of gravity were unknown before this flight into space. For this reason, a computer system had been installed to steer the spacecraft in case Gagarin was unable to. He also experimented with eating and drinking in space. Without gravity, liquid floats off in globules. It is impossible

cosmonaut: A Russian astronaut.

globules: Tiny balls of liquid.

to drink from a cup or pour water from a jug.

The prospect of reentry must have been very nerve-racking. The autopilot turned the spaceship, *Vostok 1*, around. Then it fired the retro-rocket to take Gagarin out of orbit and to slow the descent. In two of the five test flights, the retro-rockets had failed. But this one worked. *Vostok 1* came out of orbit. Gagarin could see flames on the outside of the capsule as it went through Earth's atmosphere. Then *Vostok 1* thudded onto the hard ground of Siberia.

Before Gagarin, no one had seen Earth from space. "I could clearly discern the outlines of continents, islands, and rivers. . . . A delicate blue halo surrounds the earth, merging with the blackness of space in which the stars are bright and clear-cut." *Vostok 1* circled Earth once. The whole trip was over in 108 minutes.

The Space Race

In 1961, President John F. Kennedy committed the United States to an ambitious goal. He said that within the decade the United States would put a man on the moon and bring him safely home.

discern: See and understand.

In 1969, the lunar module *Eagle* landed on the moon. As astronaut Neil Armstrong stepped onto the moon, he said these famous words: "That's one small step for man, one giant leap for mankind." Astronaut Buzz Aldrin was the second man on the moon. Armstrong and Aldrin walked around on the lunar surface collecting samples and taking photos.

Armstrong got his pilot's license when he was 16 years old, even before he got a driver's license. He was among the second group of astronaut trainees accepted by the National Aeronautics and Space Administration (NASA). On a space flight in 1966, Armstrong proved he could be calm in a crisis. A rocket failed, and he was forced to make a crash landing in the ocean.

Television brought the first days of space travel and the landing on the moon directly into people's homes. In a way, many people felt personally involved in space exploration. The moon landing captured the imagination of the world.

lunar: Of or relating to the moon.

Modern Space Travelers

In 1977, Sally Kristen Ride joined NASA to become an astronaut. The training included parachute jumping, water survival, gravity and weightlessness training, radio communications, and navigation. In 1983, Sally Ride became the first American woman in space. During two space missions, Ride spent 343 hours in space.

In 1999, Eileen Collins became the first woman to be selected to command and pilot a space shuttle. Collins was an instructor pilot and an aircraft commander in the Air Force. But she had always wanted to be an astronaut. According to Collins, it's a tough job just to get accepted into the space program. Each time interviews are held, there are about 3,000 applications from people with the right qualifications. That includes a degree in a technical area such as science, math, engineering, or medicine. Only 20 or 30 applicants are accepted to become astronauts.

The Rest of Space

So much of space is still unknown that there is no chance of running out of new worlds to explore. In 1998, a space probe discovered that there is water frozen under the moon's surface at the poles. The ice would provide a source of water and oxygen. These two elements are not readily available on the moon. The ice could also be a source of hydrogen, which could be used to make spacecraft  fuel. The moon may turn out to be our favorite launching pad.

No human has set foot on another planet. That's not to say there aren't any plans. Mars seems the most likely target for our next space landing. In 2003, NASA is planning to fly a robotic plane across inaccessible parts of the planet. It won't be a quick trip. In the type of spacecraft we have now, it will take almost nine months of space travel to reach Mars. That means the round-trip from Earth to Mars is a minimum of a year and a half. It is predicted that as early as 2020, there will be a human on Mars. Could it be you?

Where to from Here?

You've just read stories of people who risked everything to climb mountains, cross deserts, explore seas, and venture into space. Here are some ideas for learning about more awesome adventures.

The Library

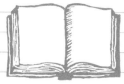

Some books you might enjoy include:
- *Arctic Explorer: The Story of Matthew Hensen* by Jeri Ferris
- *Sally Ride: Shooting for the Stars* by Jane and Sue Hurwitz
- *Within Reach, My Everest Story* by Mark Pfetzer and Jack Galvin

TV, Film, and Video

Watch TV listings for National Geographic specials such as *Surviving Everest* and *Beyond 2000: New Explorers.*

Ask at your library for videos about adventurers and explorers. Some suggestions are:
- *Into Thin Air: Death on Everest*
- *John Glenn—A True American Hero*

The Internet

Try searching the Internet using the keyword *explorer*. Check out the National Geographic site at *www.nationalgeographic.com*. Also explore *www.nasa.gov* for facts about U.S. space exploration.

People and Places

Check your library for articles in local newspapers about people who may have gone on an adventure. Find the people and see if you can interview them about their experiences.

The Ultimate Fiction Book

Be sure to check out *Crossing the Divide*, the companion volume to *Awesome Adventures*. *Crossing the Divide* tells the exciting adventure of a boy and his grandfather as they journey through treacherous mountains.

Decide for yourself where fact stops and fiction begins.

Index